Dino Digs and Ancient Things: Adventures in Archaeology A to Z

by Lacey L. Bakker

Dedicated to Denver, Harper, Harvey, and Myles

In the spirit of discovery, curiosity, and endless imagination, may your days be filled with adventures!

With love and endless possibilities,
❤ Auntie Lacey

For permission requests, contact Pandamonium Publishing House at the address below.
Pandamonium Publishing House
Email: pandapublishing8@gmail.com
Website: pandamoniumpublishing.com

First Edition, 2024
Cover Design and Interior design by Lacey L. Bakker, images from stock photos
ISBN: 978-1-989506-96-7
Printed in the USA

This book belongs to:

_____

A is for **Archaeology.** It's like being a detective for the past. Imagine you have a time machine, but instead of traveling through time, you dig into the ground to find clues about how people and animals lived long, long ago. Archaeologists study old objects, like pottery, tools, and even bones, to learn about ancient civilizations and the cool things they did. It's like putting together a big jigsaw puzzle from the past to understand our history better!

B

B is for **Bones** in the exciting world of archaeology! When archaeologists dig into the ground, they often find bones—remnants of animals or even humans from a long time ago. These bones are like time capsules, holding secrets about the creatures that once lived on Earth. By carefully studying these ancient bones, archaeologists can learn about the size, shape, and habits of animals from the past. It's like playing detective with the skeletons of creatures that roamed our world a very long time ago!

C is for **Ceramics**! In archaeology, ceramics are special objects made from clay, like pots, bowls, or even cups. These ancient creations are like treasures, telling stories about how people used to cook, eat, and store things. Archaeologists carefully study these ceramic artifacts to understand the daily lives and traditions of people from the past. It's like discovering a time-traveling kitchen and learning about the unique ways ancient civilizations crafted and used their pottery!

D is for **Dinosaurs**, the giants of the ancient world! In archaeology, scientists called paleontologists study dinosaurs, but they're like cousins to archaeologists who explore human history. Dinosaurs once roamed the Earth millions of years ago, leaving behind fascinating clues like fossilized bones and footprints. Archaeologists sometimes work with paleontologists to unlock the mysteries of these incredible creatures, piecing together the story of a time when colossal dinosaurs ruled the land. It's like going on a dino adventure through the past, discovering the incredible world they lived in!

E is for **Earth**, the ultimate archaeological playground! Archaeologists dig into the Earth to uncover treasures from the past. Every layer of soil holds clues about the people, animals, and plants that lived long ago. It's like turning the pages of a giant history book, with each layer telling a different chapter of our planet's story. The Earth is a time capsule, and archaeologists are like detectives, carefully excavating to reveal the secrets hidden beneath the surface.

F is for **Fossils**, the ancient treasures buried in the Earth! Fossils are the remains or traces of plants, animals, or even dinosaurs from long, long ago. Imagine finding a dinosaur bone or a prehistoric leaf perfectly preserved in stone. Archaeologists study these fossils to learn about the incredible creatures that once roamed our planet. It's like discovering a time capsule that allows us to peek into the distant past and understand the amazing life forms that lived before us. Fossils, the fantastic fragments of history hidden beneath the ground!

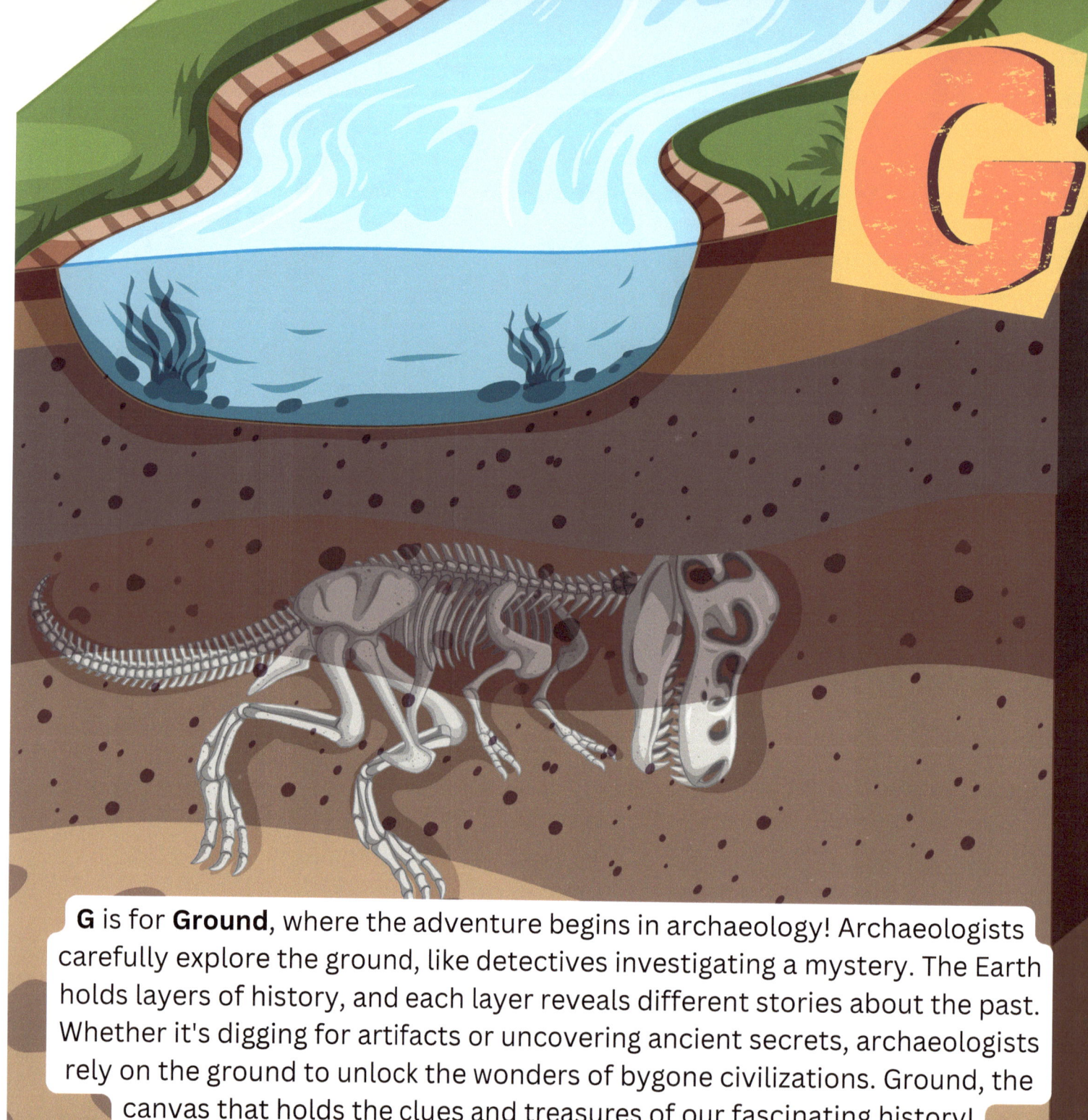

G is for **Ground**, where the adventure begins in archaeology! Archaeologists carefully explore the ground, like detectives investigating a mystery. The Earth holds layers of history, and each layer reveals different stories about the past. Whether it's digging for artifacts or uncovering ancient secrets, archaeologists rely on the ground to unlock the wonders of bygone civilizations. Ground, the canvas that holds the clues and treasures of our fascinating history!

H is for **H**istory, the incredible tale of our past! In archaeology, history is like a puzzle waiting to be solved. Archaeologists piece together the stories of ancient people by studying artifacts, bones, and structures buried in the ground. It's like reading a book written by our ancestors, learning about their cultures, daily lives, and the challenges they faced. History, a captivating journey through time that archaeologists unveil with every carefully excavated discovery!

I is for **Ice Age**, a frosty chapter in Earth's history! During the Ice Age, massive sheets of ice covered parts of the planet, shaping the landscape and influencing the creatures that lived. Archaeologists explore the remnants of this frozen era, uncovering fossils, tools, and even ancient artwork left by early humans. It's like stepping into a chilly time machine, discovering how our ancestors adapted to the challenges of icy environments. Ice Age, a frosty adventure for archaeologists unraveling the mysteries of the ancient cold!

J is for **Jurassic**, a thrilling period in Earth's past! The Jurassic period was a time when colossal dinosaurs ruled the land, and archaeologists, especially paleontologists, delve into this ancient era to uncover the secrets of these incredible creatures. Fossilized bones, footprints, and even ancient plants tell the story of a world filled with massive predators and gentle giants. It's like going on a Jurassic journey through time, exploring the wonders of a prehistoric landscape.

K is for **Kiln**, a fascinating tool in the world of archaeology! A kiln is like a special oven used by ancient people to fire and harden clay, transforming it into pottery and other ceramic artifacts. Archaeologists uncover these kilns during their digs, providing insights into the craftsmanship and techniques of past civilizations. It's like discovering the ancient "kitchens" where people baked their creations, leaving behind a legacy of beautifully crafted objects for us to admire today.

L is for **Lithics**, the fascinating study of stone tools in archaeology! Imagine delving into the ancient past, where skilled artisans crafted tools from rocks, shaping them into arrowheads, knives, and other implements essential for survival. Lithics unravels the story of human innovation and adaptation, providing insights into the daily lives and technological advancements of past civilizations.

M is for **Midden**! A midden is like an ancient trash pile where people discarded their waste, providing a rich source of information for archaeologists. By studying middens, archaeologists learn about what people ate, used, and discarded in the past. It's like discovering a time capsule of daily life, where broken pottery, bones, and other artifacts tell the story of ancient communitie

N is for **Nomads**, ancient wanderers of the past! Nomads were people who didn't settle in one place but moved from one location to another in search of food, water, and better living conditions. Archaeologists uncover evidence of nomadic lifestyles through artifacts like tools, tents, and campfire remains. It's like piecing together the journey of these adventurous groups, understanding how they adapted to different environments and left their mark on the landscapes they traversed.

O is for **Obsidian**, a fascinating archaeological find! Obsidian is a type of volcanic glass that ancient people used to create sharp tools and weapons. Archaeologists uncover obsidian artifacts during excavations, helping them trace trade routes, understand tool-making techniques, and piece together ancient economies. It's like discovering the ancient "cutting-edge" technology that our ancestors relied on for survival.

P

P is for **Paleontology**, the thrilling cousin of archaeology! While archaeologists explore the human past, paleontologists focus on ancient life, especially dinosaurs and other prehistoric creatures. They dig up fossils, study bones, and reconstruct the incredible stories of the Earth's distant inhabitants. It's like going on a fossil-filled adventure, unlocking the mysteries of creatures that roamed the planet millions of years ago.

Q is for **Quarry**, an important place in the world of archaeology and paleontology! A quarry is like a giant outdoor treasure trove where scientists excavate rocks, fossils, and artifacts. It's a source of valuable clues about Earth's history, providing a window into ancient landscapes and the creatures that inhabited them. Archaeologists and paleontologists often work in quarries, carefully extracting and studying the remnants of our planet's past.

R is for **Radiocarbon Dating**, a powerful tool in the hands of archaeologists! Radiocarbon dating is like a time-traveling clock that helps scientists determine the age of ancient objects and fossils. By measuring the amount of a radioactive form of carbon in a sample, archaeologists can estimate how long it's been since the living organism or artifact was once a part of the living world. It's like having a time machine that allows us to put a specific date on the events and objects of our archaeological discoveries.

S is for **Symbolism** in archaeology, the study of meaningful symbols left behind by ancient cultures. From intricate carvings on artifacts to symbolic depictions in art, understanding symbolism provides insights into the beliefs, rituals, and cultural expressions of past societies. Unraveling these symbolic messages allows archaeologists to piece together the rich tapestry of meaning that shaped the worldview of our ancestors

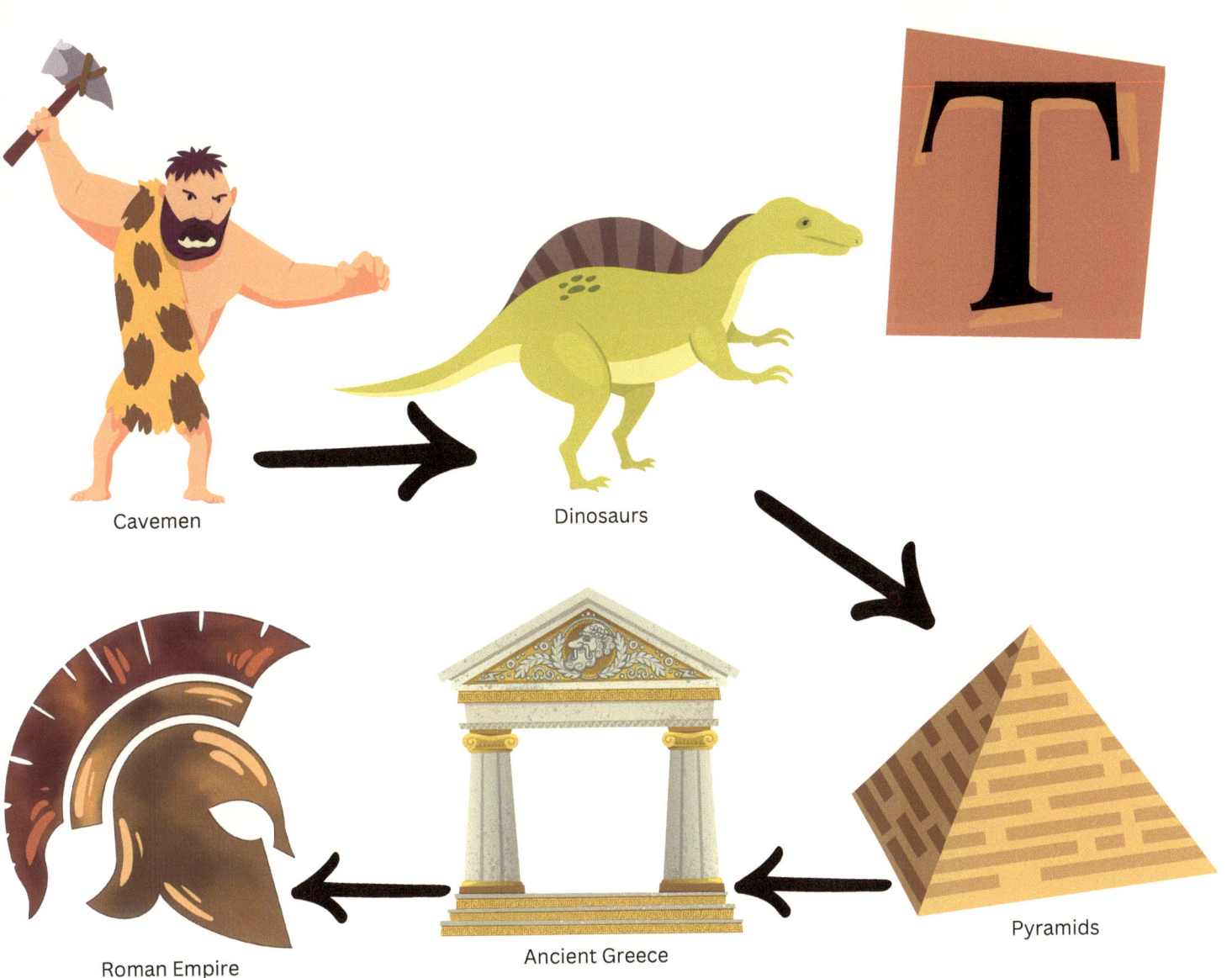

Cavemen

Dinosaurs

Pyramids

Roman Empire

Ancient Greece

T is for **Timeline**, a fantastic way to organize and understand the order of events in archaeology! Imagine a giant scroll that stretches through time, marking important moments in history. Archaeologists use timelines to piece together the puzzle of the past, placing discoveries and ancient civilizations in the right order. It's like a map of time that helps us explore and learn about the incredible stories hidden beneath the layers of history.

U is for **Urns**, ancient vessels that hold stories from the past! Urns are like beautifully crafted containers made by past civilizations to store ashes, food, or other precious items. Archaeologists find these urns during excavations, providing insights into burial practices and cultural traditions. It's like unlocking a treasure chest filled with the artifacts of ancient rituals, connecting us to the people who lived long ago.

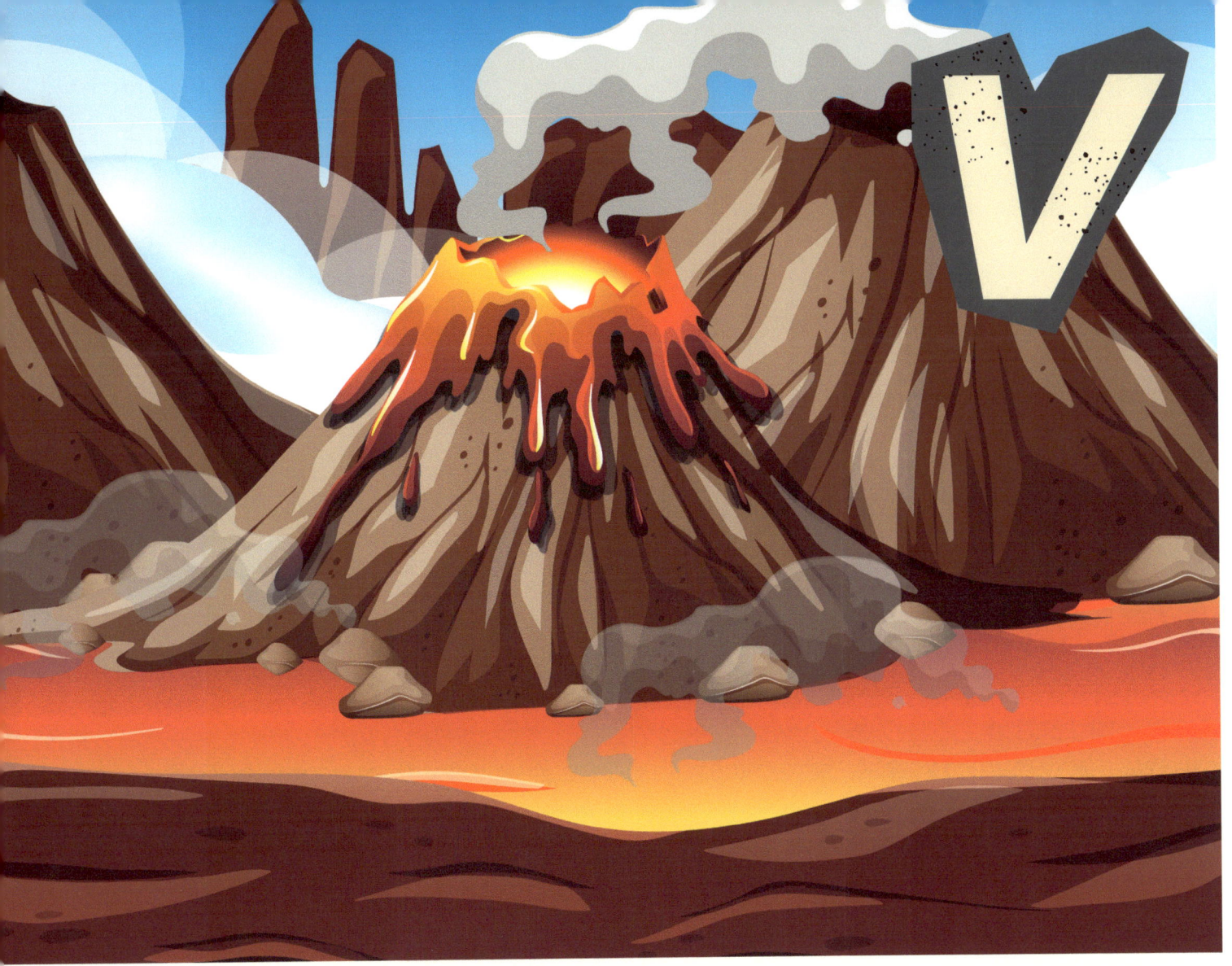

V is for **Volcano**, a powerful force shaping the archaeological landscape! Volcanoes, like fiery giants, have erupted throughout history, leaving behind layers of ash and rock. Archaeologists uncover artifacts and fossils in volcanic deposits, preserving a snapshot of life from ancient times. It's like exploring a time capsule set in stone, revealing the impact of volcanic eruptions on the people and creatures of the past.

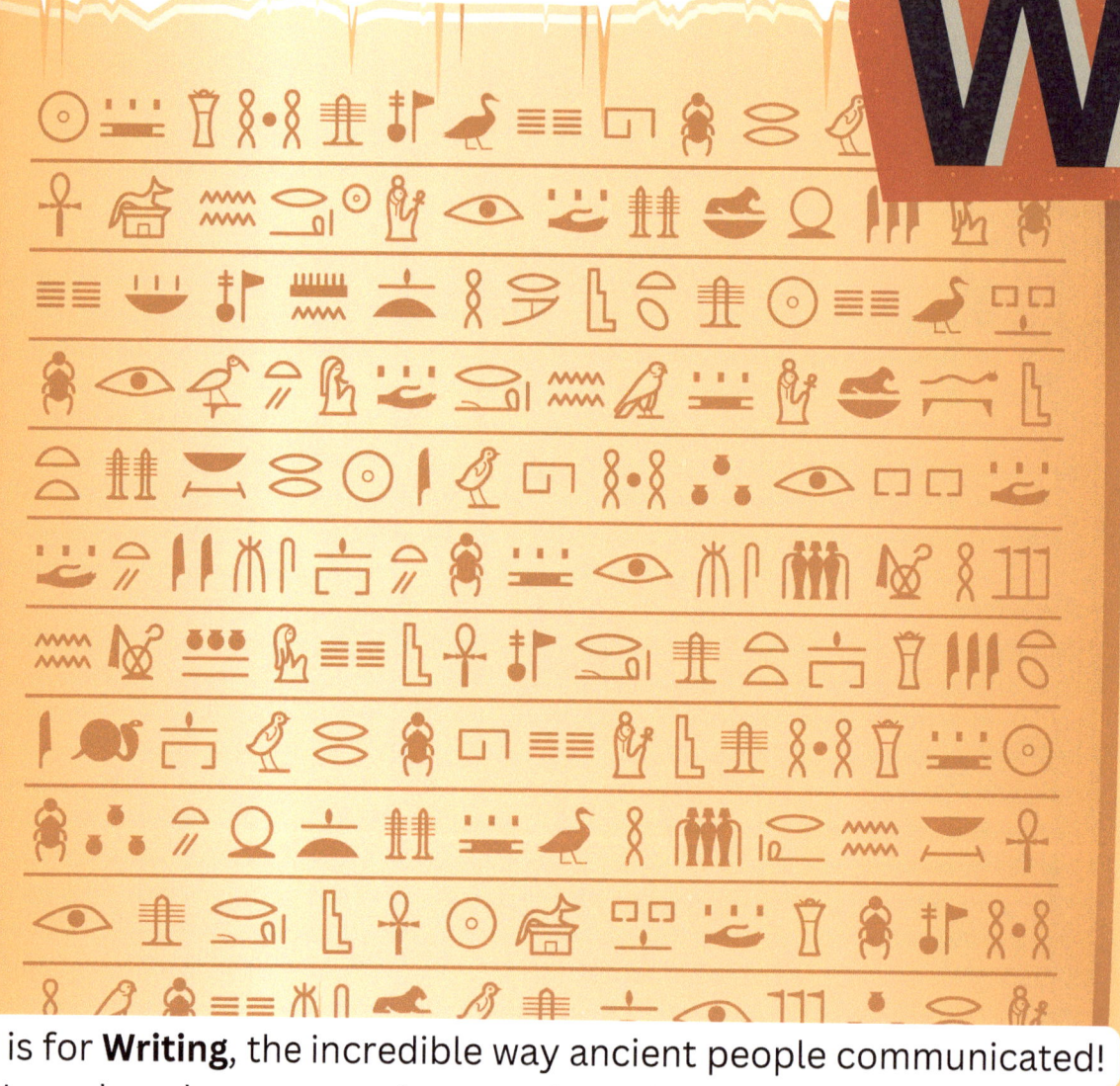

W is for **Writing**, the incredible way ancient people communicated! In archaeology, researchers study ancient writings carved into stones, etched onto pottery, or even written on papyrus. These inscriptions tell stories, convey beliefs, and document historical events. It's like deciphering the messages from the past, giving us a window into the thoughts and cultures of our ancestors.

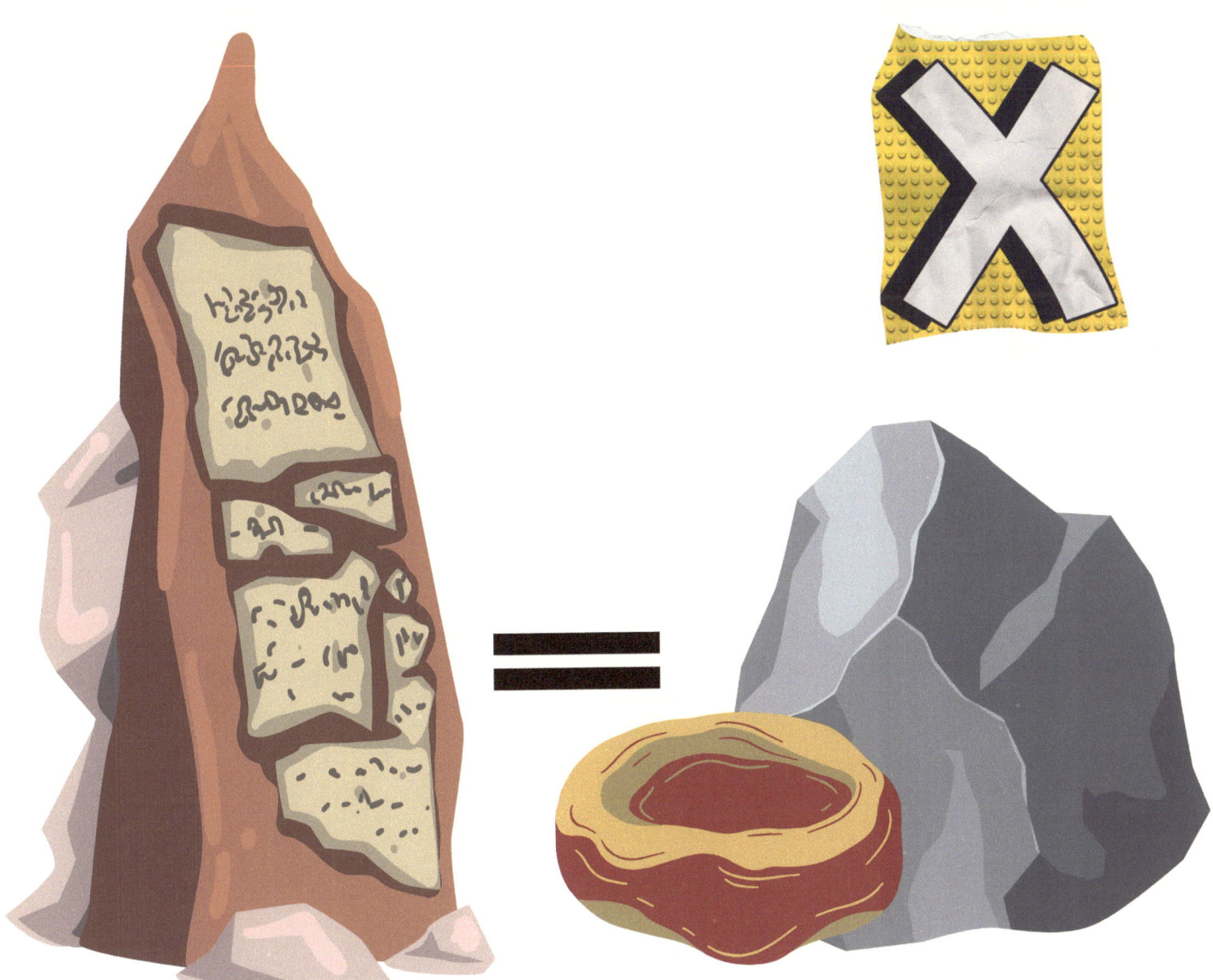

X is for **X-ray Fluorescence (XRF)**, a powerful tool in archaeology! XRF is like a high-tech detective, allowing scientists to analyze the elemental composition of artifacts without damaging them. By shooting X-rays at an object, archaeologists can determine the types of materials used, providing crucial insights into ancient technologies and trade networks. It's like a modern-day magic wand, revealing the hidden chemical signatures of the past.

Y is for **Yarn**, a thread connecting us to the past! Archaeologists sometimes find ancient textiles, woven from yarn, providing insights into the clothing, decorations, and even daily life of people in ancient civilizations. It's like unraveling a fabric tapestry that links us to the craftsmanship and creativity of our ancestors.

Z is for **Zenith**, the highest point in archaeological exploration! Archaeologists aim for the zenith when they uncover the most significant artifacts or make groundbreaking discoveries that reshape our understanding of the past. It's like reaching the pinnacle of a historical journey, where every find contributes to the mosaic of human history.

Did you know?

Did you know that some dinosaurs, like the Velociraptor, had feathers?

Did you know that archaeologists once found a 2,000-year-old piece of bubblegum in Finland? Imagine chewing on ancient gum!

Did you know that ancient Egyptians believed in the afterlife and buried their cats with them, thinking they'd need them in the next world?

Did you know that the world's oldest board game, called "Senet," was played by ancient Egyptians over 5,000 years ago?

Did you know that archaeologists have found evidence of people using toothpaste as far back as 5000 BC? Ancient smiles needed care too!

Did you know that some ancient civilizations used crushed insects to create vibrant colors for their artwork? Talk about DIY paint!

Did you know that the world's oldest toy is a doll that's over 4,000 years old?

Did you know that the largest dinosaur footprints ever discovered are as big as a bathtub?

Did you know that there's a fossil called "Tiktaalik" that's like a fish with legs? It's a missing link showing how animals transitioned from water to land!

Color the Dinosaur!

If you liked this book, you may enjoy Dinosaur Dentist! Check out a bookstore near you or order online!

About the Author

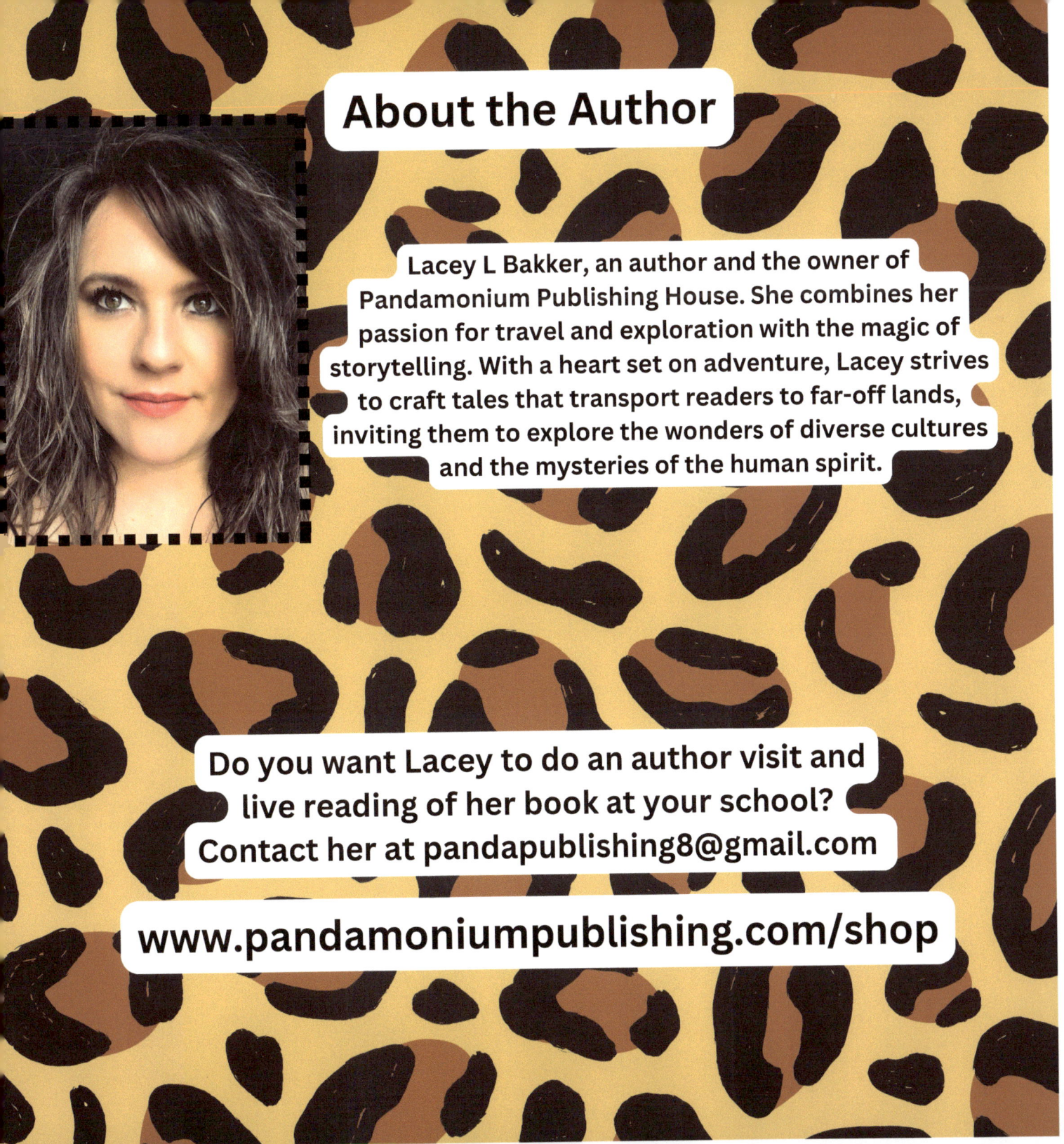

Lacey L Bakker, an author and the owner of Pandamonium Publishing House. She combines her passion for travel and exploration with the magic of storytelling. With a heart set on adventure, Lacey strives to craft tales that transport readers to far-off lands, inviting them to explore the wonders of diverse cultures and the mysteries of the human spirit.

Do you want Lacey to do an author visit and live reading of her book at your school?
Contact her at pandapublishing8@gmail.com

www.pandamoniumpublishing.com/shop

www.ingramcontent.com/pod-product-compliance
Lightning Source LLC
Chambersburg PA
CBHW041441120626
46547CB00002B/290